BULLETIN BOARDS

George F. Horn

REINHOLD BOOK CORPORATION
A subsidiary of Chapman-Reinhold, Inc.
New York   Amsterdam   London

© 1962, Reinhold Publishing Corporation
All rights reserved
Printed in the United States of America
Library of Congress Catalog Card Number 62-9142
Fifth Printing, 1968

Designed by George Horn
Printed by The Comet Press, Inc.
Bound by A. Horowitz & Son
Published by Reinhold Book Corporation
A subsidiary of Chapman-Reinhold, Inc.
430 Park Avenue, New York, N.Y. 10022

There is an old saying that people often "can't see the forest for the trees." The same thing could be said about bulletin boards. We sometimes concentrate so hard on what stares us in the face that we lose sight of the fundamentals that can be most important to us.

It is a very human trait, this blindness to what may be of greatest importance. Good teachers have recognized it for years, and in planning their instructional activities they have capitalized on it. They know that in order to communicate knowledge they must first create a thirst for it.

Pestalozzi once remarked that, "the only effective learning is that which is accomplished in the presence of reality."

Realistic learning opportunities take on many different forms in the modern school. They include the field trip and well organized textbooks handsomely illustrated with the realities of the stories they contain. Filmstrips and motion picture documentaries that capture slices of reality by displaying the means through which nature unfolds its wonders have universal appeal. But for timely and practical instructional needs the bulletin board has no equal.

This book is about bulletin boards.

Our advancing technology, the exploration of space, the race with Russia for intellectual leadership make it increasingly apparent that a high value must be placed on the acquisition of great quantities of knowledge in the years ahead. In the current efforts to improve the quality of education and to modernize instruction, teachers everywhere are seeking to improve their ability to bring reality to the learning situation. Good teachers know from experience that bulletin boards, visual displays and exhibits when properly arranged enhance learning by creating a genuine thirst for it. The bulletin board can be one of the fundamental tools of instructional realism when used properly.

George Horn is a realist. He is also a good teacher. He is constantly striving to help other teachers improve their own capabilities whereby in turn they might use their talents to enrich the lives of others. His delightful narrative explanation of processes and techniques combined with a series of clever illustrations provides a practical and meaningful approach to the use of bulletin boards as an effective teaching tool.

This publication has empirical value—being as helpful to business and industrial leaders as to educators. To any person desiring to communicate through the medium of the bulletin board, following the practical suggestions contained in this publication will help to avoid hiding worthy ideas behind the confusion of the "trees in the forest" so characteristic of typical bulletin board displays.

GEORGE B. BRAIN
Superintendent of Public Instruction
Baltimore Public Schools

My thanks to Richard L. Micherdzinski, Director of Art Education, Baltimore Public Schools, for his careful evaluation, constructive criticism and guidance in developing some of the techniques included in this book.

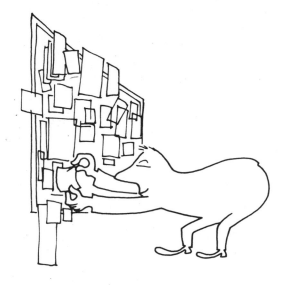

CONTENTS

Check Your Bulletin Boards   6

Tools and Materials   10

Organizing Materials to be Displayed   13

Lettering   15

Raising Flat Work   21

Displaying 3-Dimensional Objects   23

Background Shapes   26

Titles and Descriptive Matter   30

Color   33

Controlling Movement   41

Focal Points   44

Expanding the Bulletin Board   46

Linking Separate Bulletin Boards   49

Layout   52

CHECK YOUR BULLETIN BOARDS

One of the most valuable, but most neglected and misused teaching devices, is the bulletin board. Check your bulletin boards to see if you are taking full advantage of this means for visual communication. When effectively done they can make your classroom program vital, exciting, and interesting.

Do your bulletin boards cultivate . . .

blank stares?

casual glances?

--- or eyes filled with excitement?

Carefully designed bulletin boards are of immeasurable value to the teacher in building student interest. They can be used:

- To provide an overview of the semester's work. This enables the student to understand how each day's work fits into a larger plan.

- To present a single lesson.

- To explain a specific part of a lesson—a process, technique, problem.

- To display materials related to the lesson.

- To display student work over an extended period of time.

- To display student work temporarily for criticism and evaluation.

- To develop a center of continuing interest.

- To present routine notices and announcements.

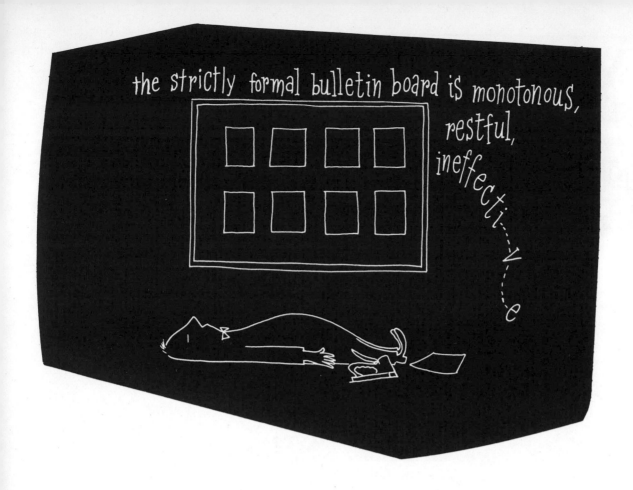

But an informal arrangement of materials tends to stimulate, excite, and raise interest, thus creating a challenging atmosphere in the room.

Where standard bulletin board facilities are not available, ingenuity plus effort can usually solve the problem. Therefore, the absence of built-in bulletin board facilities should never be an excuse for not displaying visual materials.

ONE SOLUTION:

A 4′ x 8′ piece of homosote board (Inexpensive and can be purchased in any building supply store.)
(A large piece of corrugated board from a mattress box would serve equally well.)

A 1″x 3″x 8′ strip of wood nailed across the top.
Two large screw eyes placed about 6′ apart.
Two hooks, the same distance apart, in the wood strip framing the blackboard.

Hang the bulletin board and arrange the design on it. (Display materials can be easily tacked or stapled to homosote and corrugated board, and easily removed.)

ANOTHER SOLUTION:

A section of "Peg" board or "Hole" board set out ½″ from the wall. There are standard brackets and clips for this board which can be used for display of both flat and 3-D work.

TOOLS AND MATERIALS

Scissors
Cutting Knife
Single-Edge Razor Blade
Paper Cutter
Wire Cutter
Pliers
Stapler
Colored Pencils
Pastels or Chalks
Felt-Tip Pens
Brushes
Speedball Pens
Showcard Paints
Watercolor Paints
Inks
Rubber Cement
Household Cement
Paste
Cellophane Tape

Cover Paper,
    various colors
Tissue Paper,
    various colors
Project Paper Rolls,
    various colors
Metallic Paper
Mesh
Burlap
Felt
Wire
String
Yarn
Thread
Golf Tees
Straight Pins,
    large size
Balsa Wood,
    sheets, strips

Tag Board
Poster Board
Corrugated Board
Homosote Board
Construction Paper,
    various colors

Scrap Materials

Boxes
Tubes
Corks, Bottle Caps
Buttons
Newspapers
Metal Containers
Paper Plates
Egg Cartons
Tongue Depressors
Window Blinds

When designing a bulletin board it should be kept in mind that the purpose of display material is to enhance the subject-matter being exhibited. Excessive use of display materials can be overpowering, thus diverting attention from the central theme.

One trap that the designer can easily fall into is to use an excessive amount of a single material, such as yarn, which is fun to use.

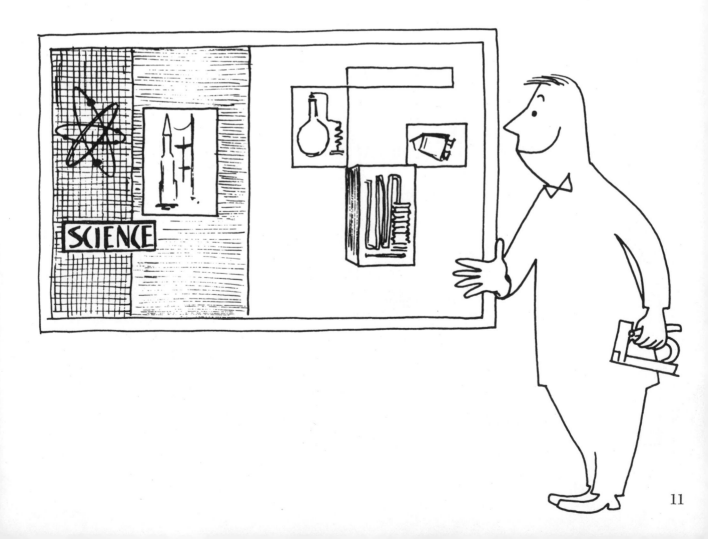

SCIENCE

Another failing is to incorporate too many different kinds of materials into one bulletin board.

A limited use of two or three different kinds of display material usually leads to more successful design. These materials may differ in color, size, and texture, but they will be effective if used with simplicity. They should always be subordinated to the material on display.

There are three basic concerns in organizing material to be displayed:

- The Title or Theme
- The Descriptive Matter
- The Visual Materials (pictures, drawings, photos, 3-dimensional objects)

After deciding on the theme, visual materials should be carefully selected, using just enough to tell the story attractively and effectively. Descriptive matter should be brief and to the point.

Photographs should usually be mounted before being displayed. First, trim off all the white edges. Then mount the photographs on poster board, or homosote board if a thicker material is desired. The edges can be painted to create greater interest.

Magazine illustrations may be cut and stapled directly to the bulletin board. However, if the illustrations are to be saved for future use, they should first be mounted on heavy paper, tag board, or poster board.

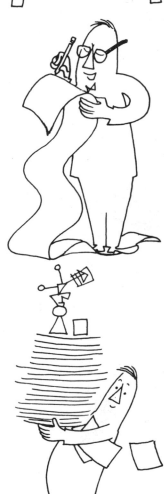

Interesting variations in photographs and illustrations can be achieved through vignetting. This is done by cutting away the background so that central objects or figures stand alone.

Dry mounting of photographs and illustrations is a most desirable technique if the equipment is available. On the other hand, excellent results in mounting can be had from using rubber cement, paste or glue.

When displaying children's work, do not attempt to include every student's work in a single bulletin board arrangement. Through frequent changes of bulletin board material, each child's work can eventually be displayed to better advantage.

A valuable aid to good bulletin board design is the development of a picture file containing illustrations covering a variety of topics. Some excellent sources for visual materials are:

- National Magazines
- Trade & Professional Journals
- Newspapers
- Folders, booklets and brochures prepared by business and industry (millions of dollars are spent each year by industry in the preparation of a wide variety of visual materials which may be obtained free upon request.)
- Commercially printed posters and product packages, book jackets, album covers.

Cut-out letters have a high degree of flexibility in the ways they can be used.

- Pasted or stapled flat onto the bulletin board or a piece of colored paper. The emphasis of a statement, or word in a statement, may be controlled by the combination of colors used. Light-colored lettering on a black background would create strong contrast. But if the importance of the lettering is to be diminished a grey background should be substituted for the black.

- Raised from the bulletin board by using pins, thus creating a 3-D effect.

- Stapled at the bottom and raised at the top with pins.

Another possibility would be to use the paper from which the letters have been cut. This negative lettering may be stapled directly to the board or to a shape of colored paper; or it may be raised on pins.

One technique assuring uniformity in size of the cut-out letters is to cut them from strips of paper that are as wide as the desired height. A variation of this would be to cut every other letter a little shorter than the strip of paper. This calculated irregularity in lettering will reflect a casual, free feeling.

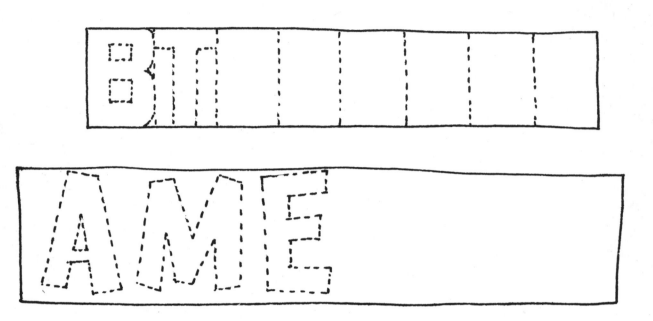

Very attractive results can be achieved with colored chalks or pastels. Letter free-hand, block or script, allowing the thickness of the chalk to determine the weight of the letter. The brilliance of pastels becomes somewhat luminescent on black paper.

Although practice and skill are generally required with brush and paint, or pen and ink, the use of these tools and materials should not be avoided. The brush can give a free, informal, flowing effect; while the pen gives a hard, mechanical-looking result, which is sometimes desired.

The felt-tip pen is manufactured in many different colors and is a fairly simple tool that brings surprising results in lettering.

Where a cutawl is available, titles may be cut from homosote board or thick cardboard. Three-D positive or negative effects can be had depending on whether the words cut out are used or the board from which they are cut.

An otherwise good bulletin board can lose much of its impact through stereotyped, timid lettering of titles and captions. This can be easily avoided by using some of the materials and techniques that have been suggested here.

Many bulletin boards are designed entirely around flat, visual material (photos, illustrations, drawings, papers, charts).

In order to avoid surface monotony, some of the flat material being displayed should be raised from the face of the bulletin board. There are numerous ways to accomplish this.

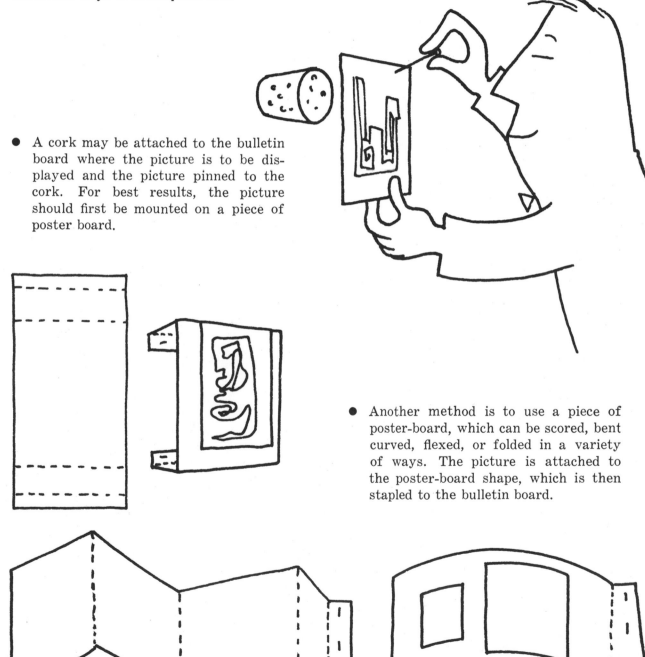

- A cork may be attached to the bulletin board where the picture is to be displayed and the picture pinned to the cork. For best results, the picture should first be mounted on a piece of poster board.

- Another method is to use a piece of poster-board, which can be scored, bent curved, flexed, or folded in a variety of ways. The picture is attached to the poster-board shape, which is then stapled to the bulletin board.

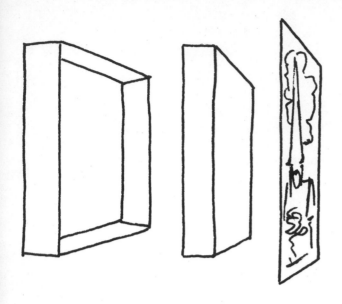

● Still another simple technique is to attach the picture to the lid of a box. Staple the box in desired position on the board. Place the lid with the picture attached, on the box.

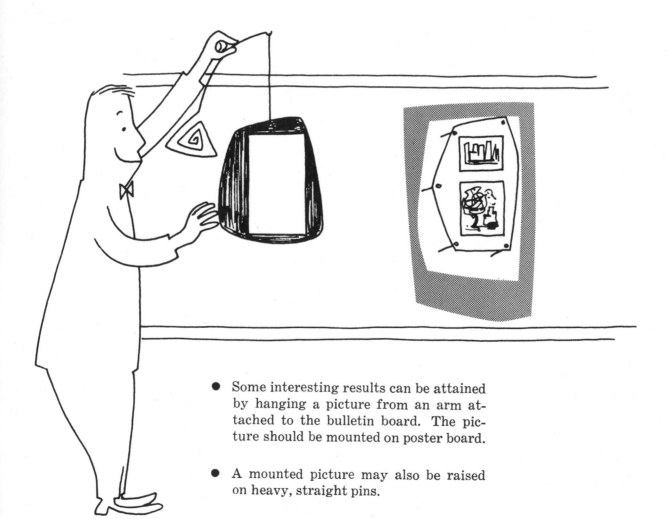

● Some interesting results can be attained by hanging a picture from an arm attached to the bulletin board. The picture should be mounted on poster board.

● A mounted picture may also be raised on heavy, straight pins.

The way in which 3-D objects are incorporated into a bulletin board design is generally dictated by the objects themselves. They may be placed on shelves, in open boxes, or they may be caged or hung.

One type of shelf can be made by scoring and folding cardboard, and adding separate cardboard supports.

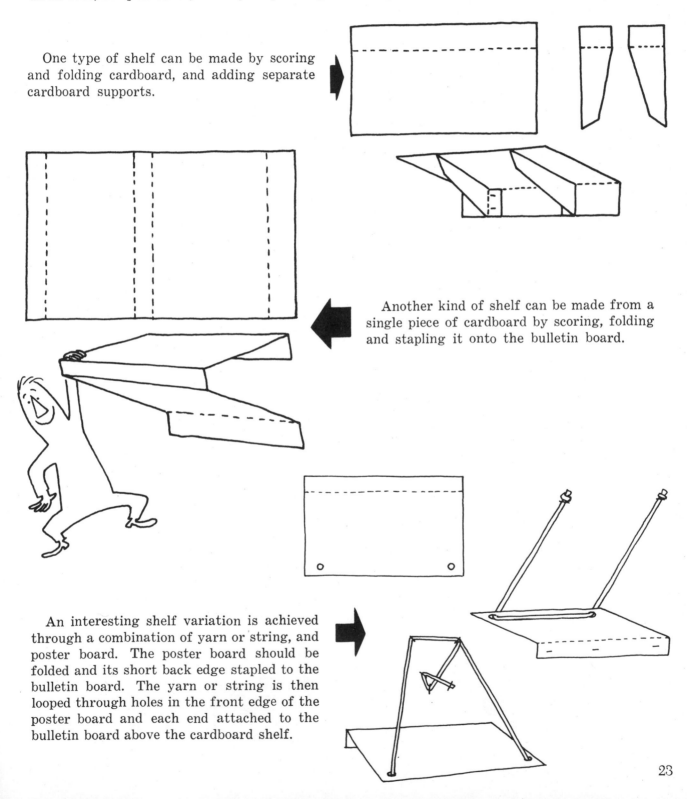

Another kind of shelf can be made from a single piece of cardboard by scoring, folding and stapling it onto the bulletin board.

An interesting shelf variation is achieved through a combination of yarn or string, and poster board. The poster board should be folded and its short back edge stapled to the bulletin board. The yarn or string is then looped through holes in the front edge of the poster board and each end attached to the bulletin board above the cardboard shelf.

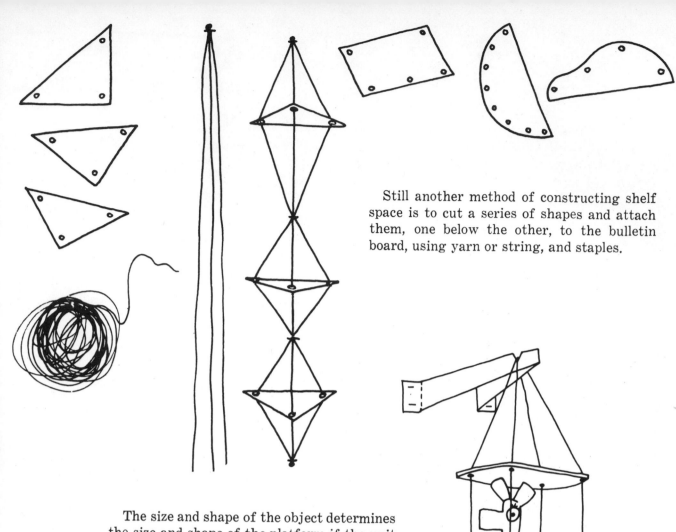

Still another method of constructing shelf space is to cut a series of shapes and attach them, one below the other, to the bulletin board, using yarn or string, and staples.

The size and shape of the object determines the size and shape of the platform if the unit is to be hung from an arm attached to the bulletin board.

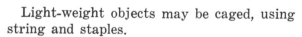

Light-weight objects may be caged, using string and staples.

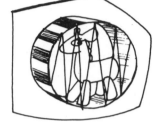

Using boxes in different ways assures continuing interest in the bulletin board. One sure-fire attention-getter is the box with a peephole through which the object or point of interest may be viewed. The top end of the box should be cut away and a covering substituted of a transparent or translucent material so that the inside of the box can receive light.

Colorfully painted boxes stapled to the bulletin board are generally very attractive for displaying 3-D items. The size of the box depends on the size of the object to be displayed. Round hat boxes offer relief from square or rectangular box shapes.

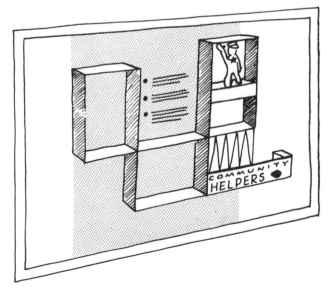

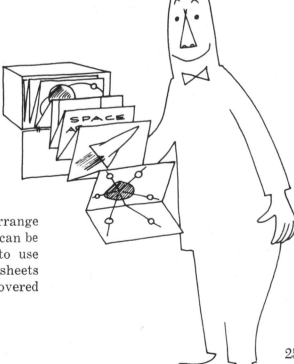

Another interesting technique is to arrange the box so that the front is hinged and can be opened out. This makes it possible to use "pop-outs" such as accordion-folded sheets containing the various points to be covered in the lesson.

BACKGROUND SHAPES

Quite often, visual material to be displayed in its own dimensions looks somewhat static and dull. Placing such material on a plain background would attract little attention.

By introducing unusual, interesting, largely abstract shapes behind static visual material, viewer-attention can be tremendously increased. The aim here is to alter the area surrounding the illustration or object on display. This may be done effectively in a seemingly infinite number of ways. However, one caution: do not use a different background shape for each of several illustrations to be included in a single display. An unusual shape behind one illustration leads the eye into the display, but too many unusual shapes cause confusion. Similar or related shapes tend to unify.

By cutting or tearing colored paper, limitless changes and variations in background are possible. Angles and triangles are fast-moving; circles, spinning; free forms, slow and ponderous. A shape may be formed to point into the illustration or to lead the eye from it to another part of the bulletin board design.

The designer should work with a high degree of flexibility in forming background shapes. The paper cut away is often a more interesting shape than the one being cut out.

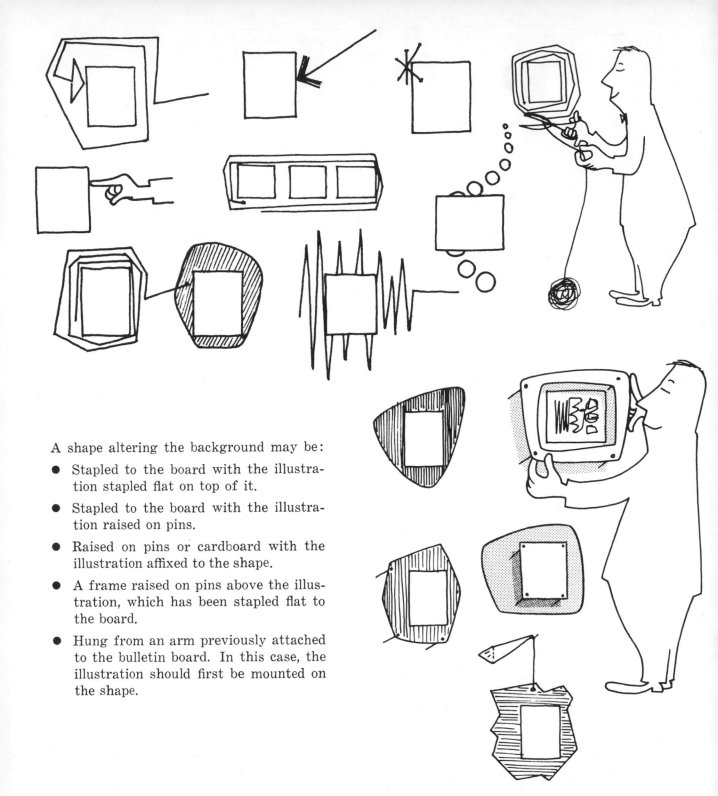

A shape altering the background may be:

- Stapled to the board with the illustration stapled flat on top of it.

- Stapled to the board with the illustration raised on pins.

- Raised on pins or cardboard with the illustration affixed to the shape.

- A frame raised on pins above the illustration, which has been stapled flat to the board.

- Hung from an arm previously attached to the bulletin board. In this case, the illustration should first be mounted on the shape.

Materials such as string, yarn, or plastic clothesline may be stapled around an illustration in different ways to make the background interesting and to enhance the illustration.

Paint and brush used freehand can also bring about interesting results.

Corrugated cardboard, cloth or wire mesh, burlap, and a variety of scrap materials lend themselves well to background effects.

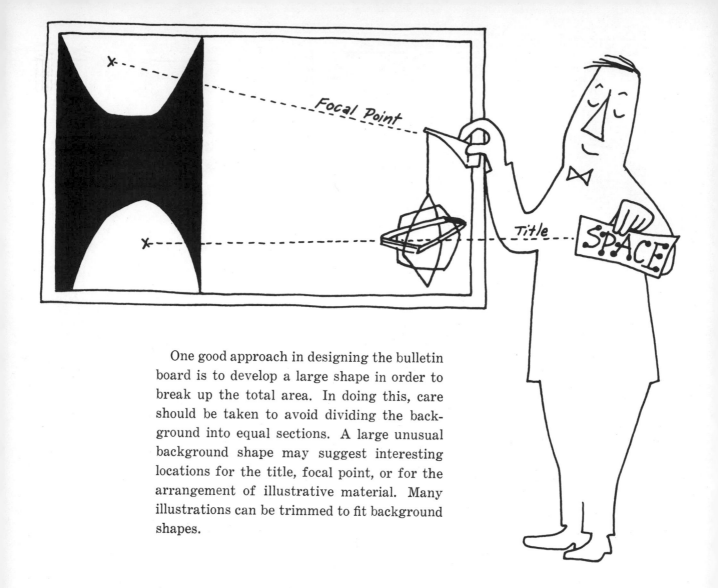

One good approach in designing the bulletin board is to develop a large shape in order to break up the total area. In doing this, care should be taken to avoid dividing the background into equal sections. A large unusual background shape may suggest interesting locations for the title, focal point, or for the arrangement of illustrative material. Many illustrations can be trimmed to fit background shapes.

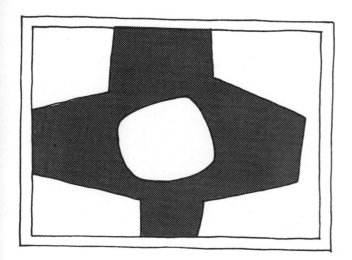

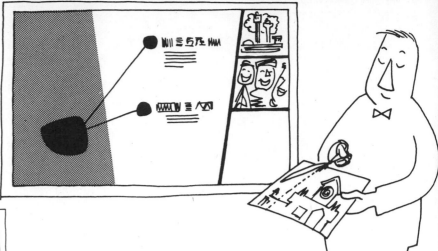

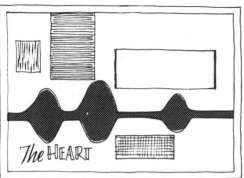

Large shapes suggested by the subject-matter or theme of a bulletin board produce attention-getting variations. Such eye-catching shapes can aid in unifying the design and serve as an exciting change.

The bulletin board designer should strive for the unusual. Uniqueness is a major criterion in successful bulletin board design.

TITLES AND DESCRIPTIVE MATTER

Titles for bulletin board displays should be brief, to the point, eye-catching. One to five carefully chosen words should be enough for most purposes. Well-designed titles require as much imagination, effort and planning as any other single phase of bulletin board design. The title should be an integral part of the total design. It can be stapled flat on the board, raised with pins, or hung from an arm to get limited movement.

The title may, in some cases, be placed outside of the bulletin board, directing attention into the design.

To achieve 3-D effects, the bulletin board designer should try the following devices:

- Staple the title to the lid of a box; staple the box to the board, then place the lid on the box.
- Fold a cardboard shape in any one of countless ways, staple it to the bulletin board and affix the title to the shape.
- Form an arm with a piece of wire. Staple the arm to the bulletin board and hang the title on it.

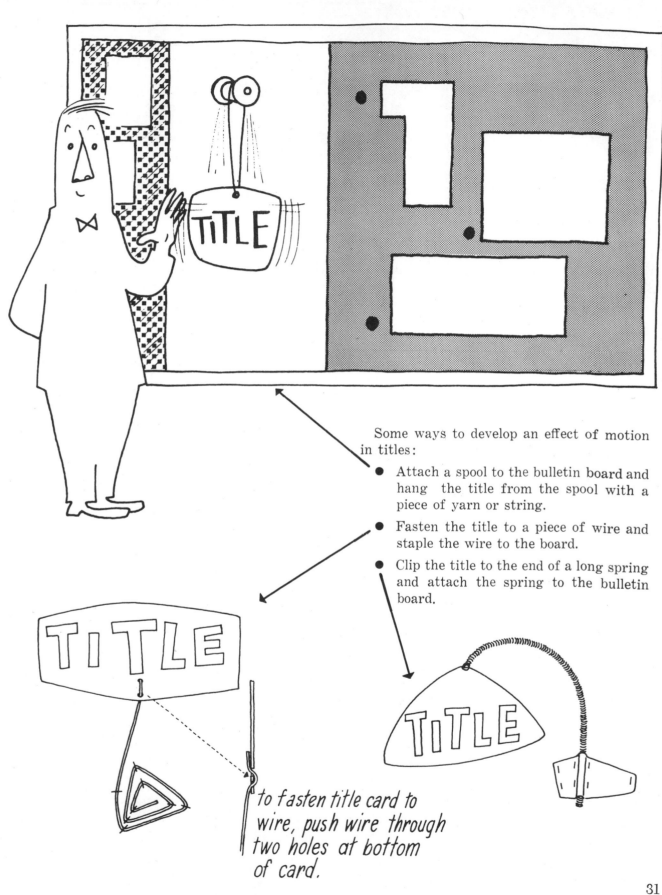

Some ways to develop an effect of motion in titles:

- Attach a spool to the bulletin board and hang the title from the spool with a piece of yarn or string.

- Fasten the title to a piece of wire and staple the wire to the board.

- Clip the title to the end of a long spring and attach the spring to the bulletin board.

to fasten title card to wire, push wire through two holes at bottom of card.

Like the title, the descriptive text should be brief and incorporated into the over-all design of the bulletin board. Such information may be lettered on a card with a speedball pen, or typed using all capital letters if possible. In most cases, descriptive matter should be located near the title for clarity and continuity.

To be effective, the use of color in bulletin board design must be carefully related to the visual material to be displayed. Color should reflect the theme. The colors used in a design should neither overpower the material on display nor fight with it. The whole color scheme should complement the idea being visually presented.

- Color is symbolic by association. For example, red often signifies heat, love, rage, or war; blue—coolness, purity; green — freshness, youth; yellow — cowardice; purple—royalty. (Only one color, green, has been shown on this page. For an example of red as a symbol of heat, see the lower-right illustration on page 36.)

● On the other hand, when used sensitively, color has great aesthetic appeal in itself. Color may be used in the background simply because it relates well to the visual material being displayed.

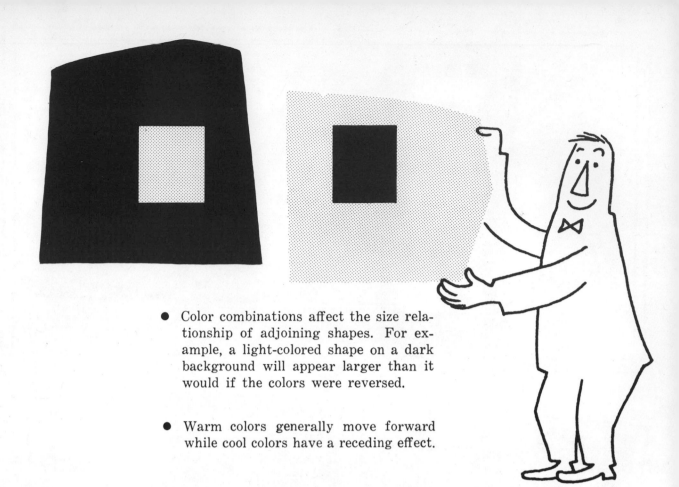

- Color combinations affect the size relationship of adjoining shapes. For example, a light-colored shape on a dark background will appear larger than it would if the colors were reversed.

- Warm colors generally move forward while cool colors have a receding effect.

Current Events

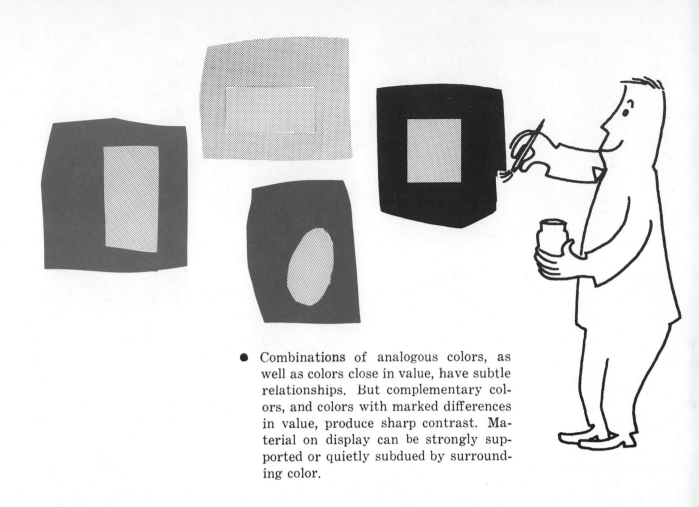

● Combinations of analogous colors, as well as colors close in value, have subtle relationships. But complementary colors, and colors with marked differences in value, produce sharp contrast. Material on display can be strongly supported or quietly subdued by surrounding color.

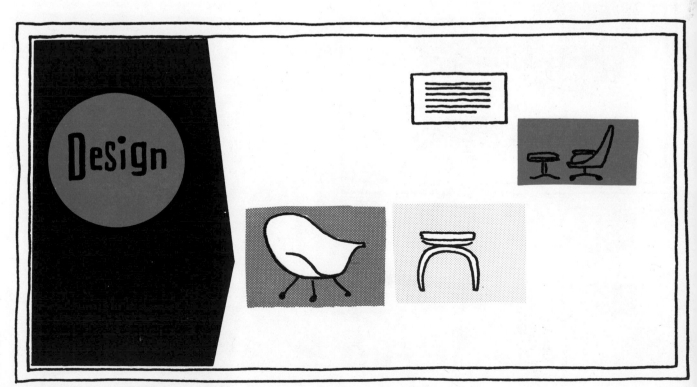

Color can be a major unifying element in bulletin board design. Several illustrations overlapping a single colored shape become an interesting unit. This feeling of unification also may be achieved with lines, panels or spots of color.

COLOR
ENHANCES

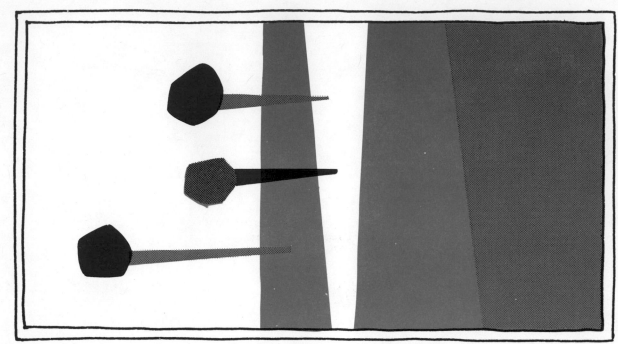

COLOR enriches

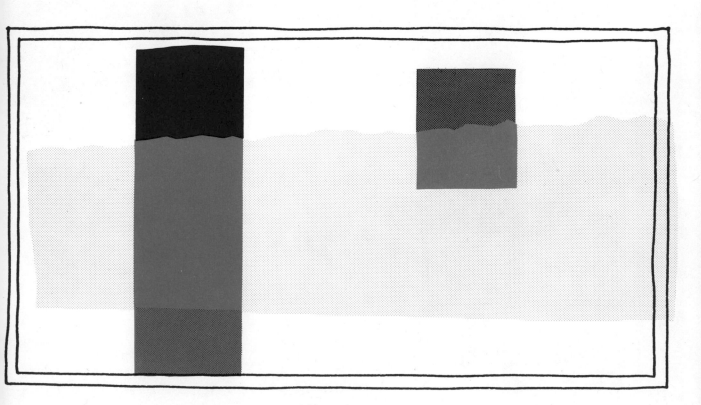

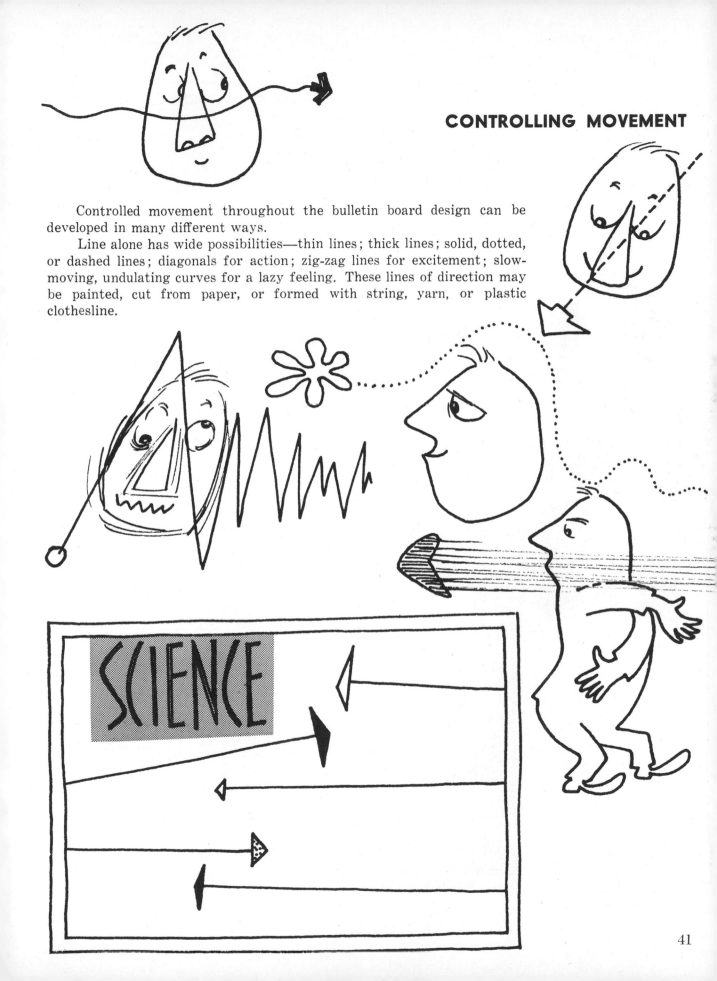

Controlled movement throughout the bulletin board design can be developed in many different ways.

Line alone has wide possibilities—thin lines; thick lines; solid, dotted, or dashed lines; diagonals for action; zig-zag lines for excitement; slow-moving, undulating curves for a lazy feeling. These lines of direction may be painted, cut from paper, or formed with string, yarn, or plastic clothesline.

SCIENCE

Movement and direction can also be achieved through the strategic placement of related shapes, colors, or through the use of positive with negative shapes.

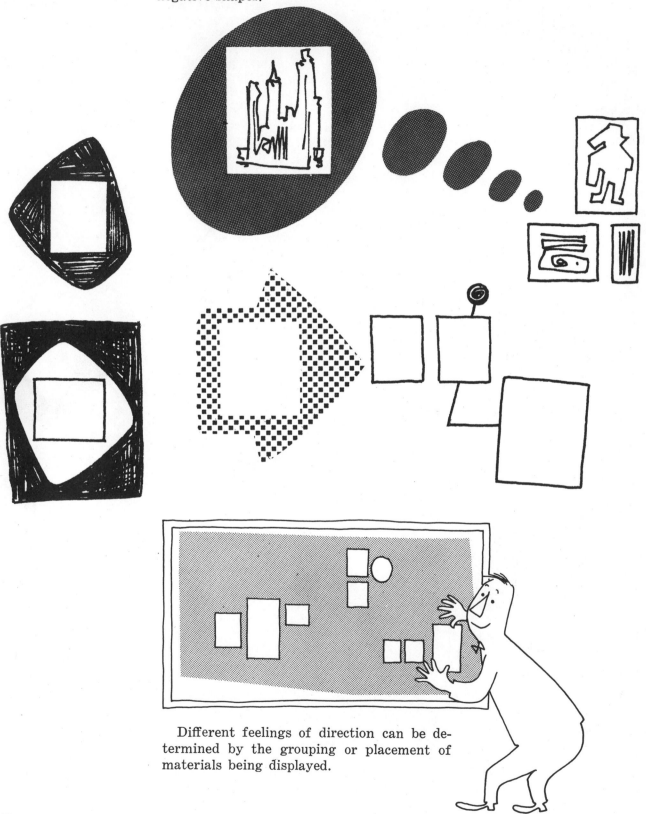

Different feelings of direction can be determined by the grouping or placement of materials being displayed.

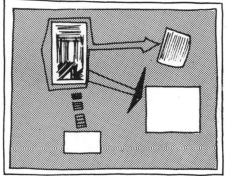

A well-organized bulletin board design should generate a feeling of systematic movement from one point to another.

FOCAL POINTS

Viewer interest in bulletin boards is perpetuated by frequent changes in technique as well as design. Thus, it is advantageous for the designer to develop various unique devices which may be employed to attract attention.

An obvious place for a startling change would be at the beginning of the "story" on display. Usually this is the spot occupied by the title. Here, the creative designer can let his imagination "take over" in the form of a three-dimensional focal point. These attention-getting contrivances should be abstract in nature and may include the title or simply lead to the title.

Although the primary purpose of such a device is to focus attention on the bulletin board, it should also reflect the spirit of the theme.

The designer may work with shapes cut from differently colored poster boards or he may use combinations of wire, balsa wood, dowels, string, colored paper, cardboard tubes, colored cellophane. Abstract designs in paper sculpture are also very effective.

The focal point may be on the bulletin board or hung from an arm attached to the bulletin board. Another variation is to place the focal point on a small table or stand near the bulletin board.

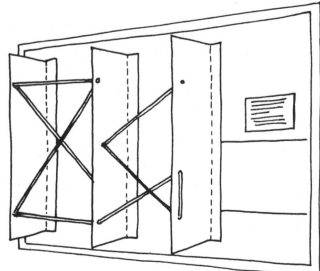

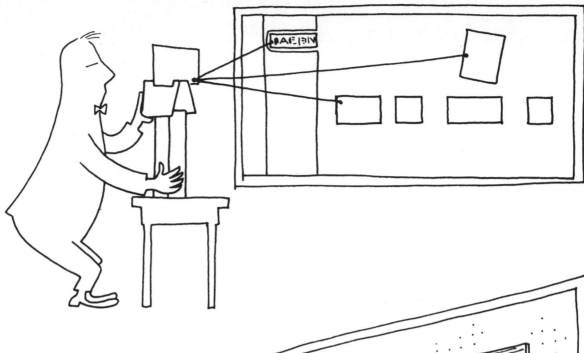

Where "hole board" is available, interesting focal points can be developed with golf tees and yarn incorporated with a single significant letter to arouse curiosity. The heads of the golf tees may be painted different colors for accent.

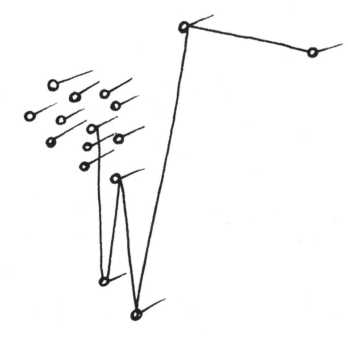

Short sections of colorfully painted cardboard tubing, or multi-color round-headed pins, can also focus attention.

EXPANDING THE BULLETIN BOARD

There may be occasions when existing bulletin board facilities are not large enough for the materials to be displayed.

This problem can be solved in a number of ways:

- Simple wings may be added to one or both ends of the bulletin board. These may be made out of poster board or corrugated box board scored, folded, and tacked to the bulletin board.

- A more elaborate arrangement would be a triangular-shaped wing—a length of poster board or corrugated box board scored in three places, folded, taped at the open end and tacked to the bulletin board. Variations on this shape can be obtained by additional scoring and folding. Shelves for 3-D objects, or arms for hanging material may be added for further interest.

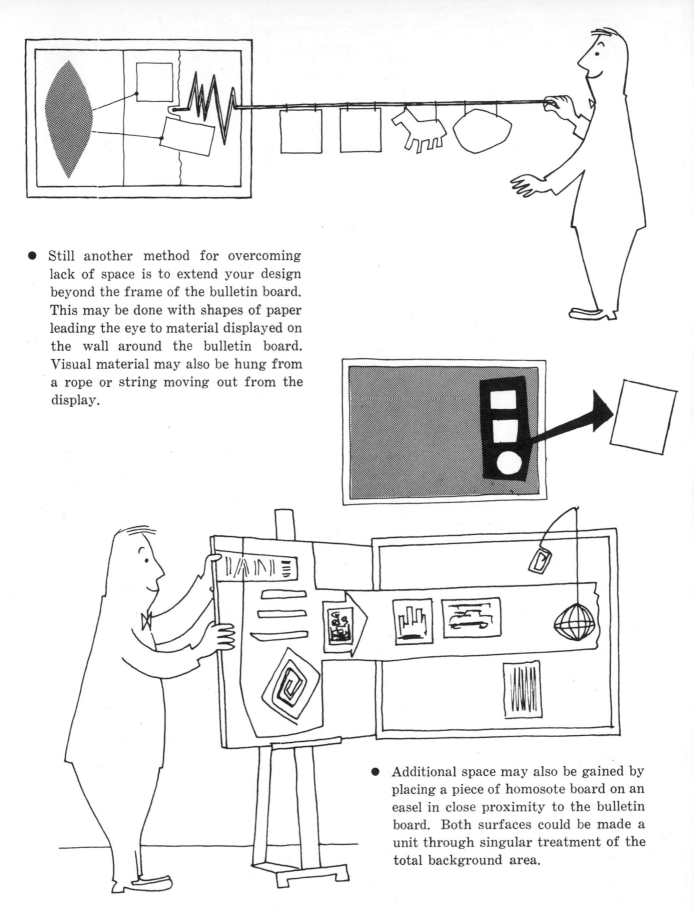

● Still another method for overcoming lack of space is to extend your design beyond the frame of the bulletin board. This may be done with shapes of paper leading the eye to material displayed on the wall around the bulletin board. Visual material may also be hung from a rope or string moving out from the display.

● Additional space may also be gained by placing a piece of homosote board on an easel in close proximity to the bulletin board. Both surfaces could be made a unit through singular treatment of the total background area.

● A variation on these solutions would be the use of a table for 3-D objects, which may be tied into the design with string or yarn. In absence of a table, a piece of homosote board makes a good shelf surface. It may be tacked to the bottom frame of the bulletin board and supported by yarn secured to the upper part of the bulletin board.

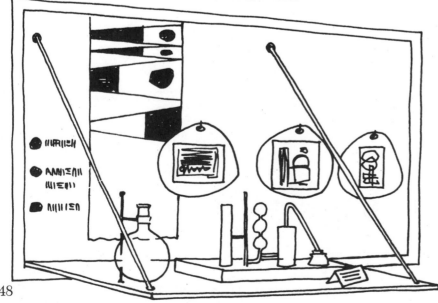

The frame around a bulletin board is no reason for restricting all display material to this pre-determined space. And when more than one bulletin board exists in a room, there may be need to tie them together into a continuing display.

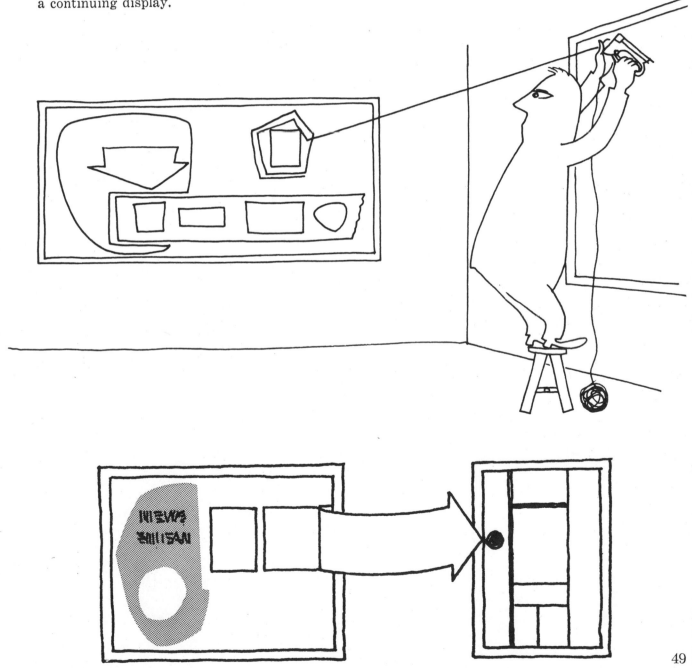

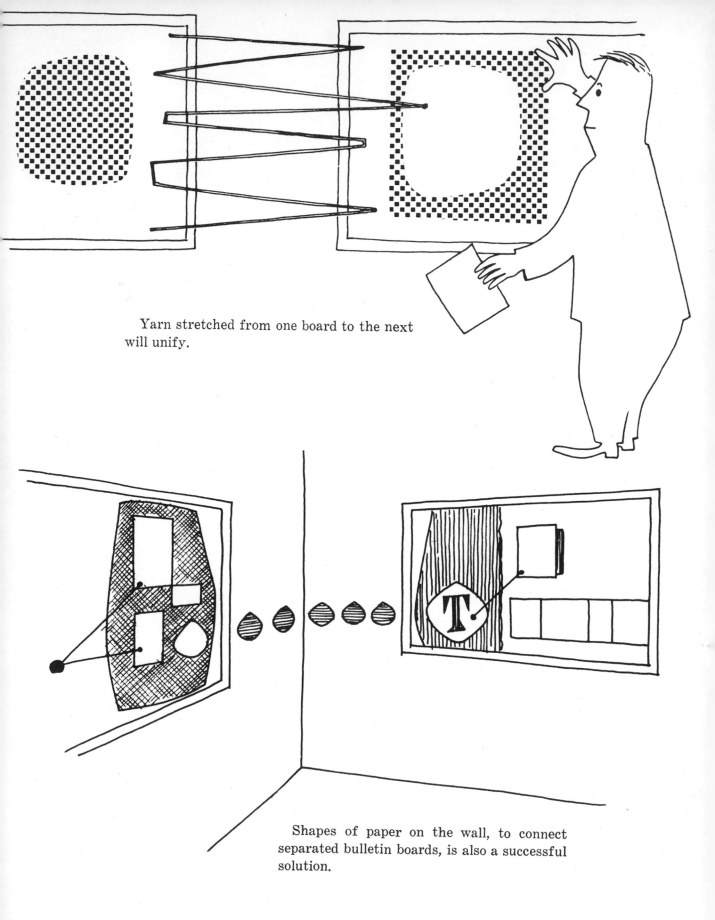

Yarn stretched from one board to the next will unify.

Shapes of paper on the wall, to connect separated bulletin boards, is also a successful solution.

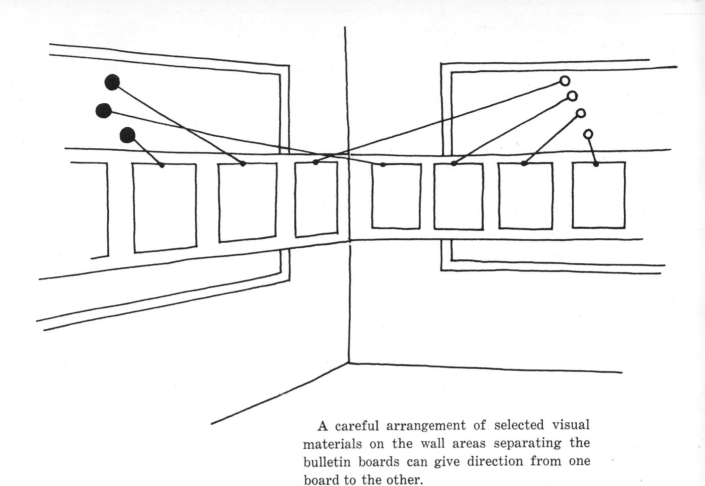

A careful arrangement of selected visual materials on the wall areas separating the bulletin boards can give direction from one board to the other.

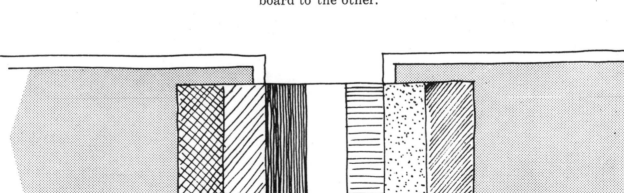

A link of multi-colored paper creates an exciting tie between separate bulletin boards.

LAYOUT

To be effective, bulletin boards must undergo frequent change. Both layout and visual material can become stale and uninteresting. So the designer must continually seek new arrangements and be cognizant of new materials, techniques and devices.

The well-designed bulletin board is the culminating product growing out of an understanding of:

- Bases for selecting display material
- The effect of color
- Movement and direction
- 3-D effects
- Background shapes
- Methods of titling and including descriptive matter
- Focal points
- Special display techniques and devices
- Tools and materials

The layouts included in this section reflect the basic points made earlier in the book.

Satisfaction with the same stereotyped arrangements kills all interest in bulletin boards.

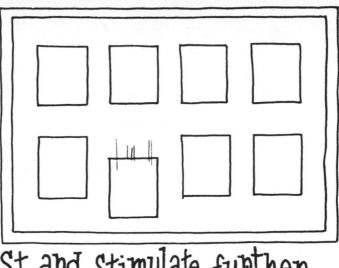

a slight alteration in layout can rekindle viewer interest and stimulate further, more interesting changes.

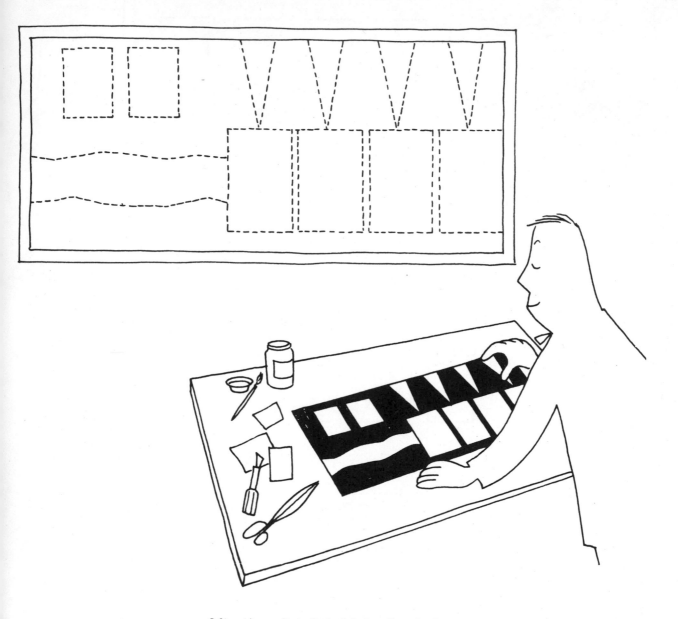

Oftentimes it is helpful for the designer to make preliminary plans on a smaller scale before completing the actual bulletin board.

One very flexible technique is outlined as follows:

- Determine the scale to be used (1/4 to 1, 1/5 to 1, 1/8 to 1, etc.)

- Cut a shape representing the bulletin board to this scale. For example, if the actual bulletin board is 4' x 8' and the scale is 1/4 to 1, then the shape would be 1' x 2'.

- Cut shapes representing illustrative material, title, descriptive matter to same scale determined from point 1.

- Move these smaller shapes around, on the larger shape representing the bulletin board, until a desirable arrangement is reached.

- Then transfer this scaled design to the full size bulletin board.

Although different combinations of illustrations, materials, techniques, and devices are as limitless as the imagination will allow, there are four basic layout approaches that should be considered.

Creating interest in a formal arrangement

By irregular application of spots of color or interesting shapes, the strictly formal layout can achieve an informal feeling. Attention can be focused on the leading illustration by combining it with a block of paper on which an eye-catching shape may be placed. More varied results can be achieved by altering the background of some of the visual materials on display.

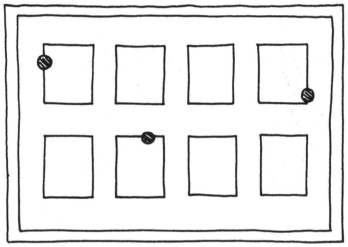

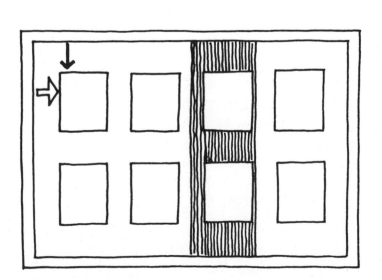

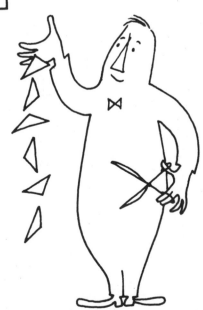

Dividing the bulletin board space with narrow strips of black paper

The designer may start with an evenly divided bulletin board. The addition of irregular color shapes will relieve the monotony of equally divided areas. As the layout develops, the visual material, title, and descriptive matter will fall into seemingly natural spots created by breaking up the background.

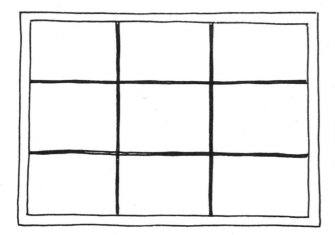 

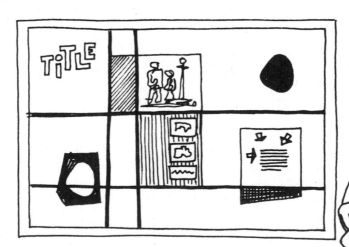

Or, narrow black strips may be placed in such a way as to provide a series of pleasing, unmonotonous spaces. Blocks of color, interesting shapes, visual material, title and descriptive matter can then be organized within these spaces.

Introducing 3-D effects

The visual material to be displayed should first be tentatively spotted, in a predetermined sequence, over the bulletin board. Best results are achieved when the arrangement reflects some type of grouping. Then the title and one or more of the illustrations may be raised to give a 3-D effect; or an added dimension can be achieved through the use of yarn. Proper treatment of the background should give further unity.

Constructing 3-D forms

Many bulletin board themes suggest 3-D forms. It is best to construct these first so that they can be included with the visual material as the bulletin board layout is being developed. The size or shape of a 3-D form often suggests the positioning of other visual material.

These approaches to bulletin board layout can be helpful to the designer. However, for increasingly better results, he must work with a high degree of flexibility. He must explore the potentials of a variety of materials and take advantage of what they suggest to him. An excellent source of ideas for arrangement of display materials, use of color, and use of lettering styles is to be found in magazine advertisements.

even notices can be interesting!

The bulletin board may first be divided into pleasing unmonotonous shapes; the title, descriptive matter, and illustrations, then added.

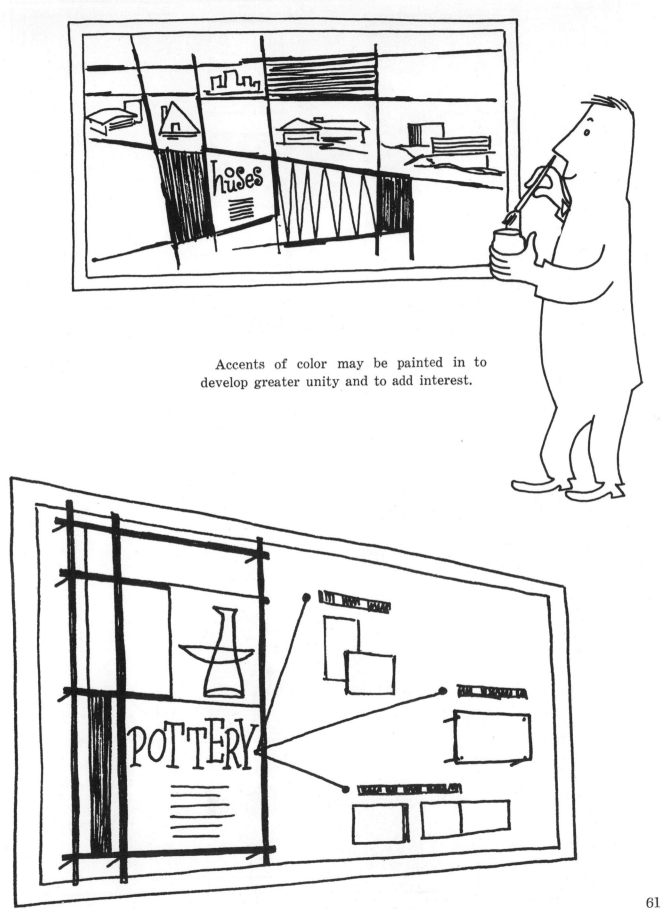

Accents of color may be painted in to develop greater unity and to add interest.

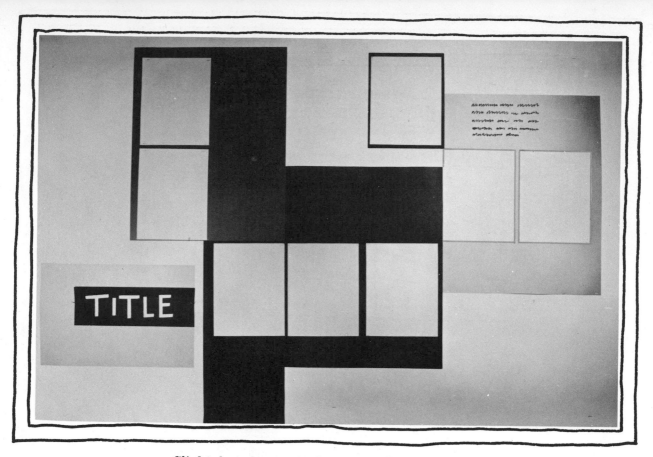

Slight but frequent changes in the same bulletin board design can retain interest over a longer period of time.

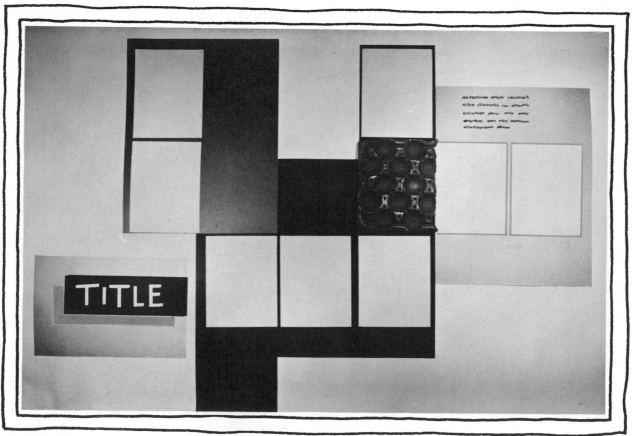

Title raised and three-dimensional shape (egg carton) added.

Title raised; colored, positive and negative shapes added.

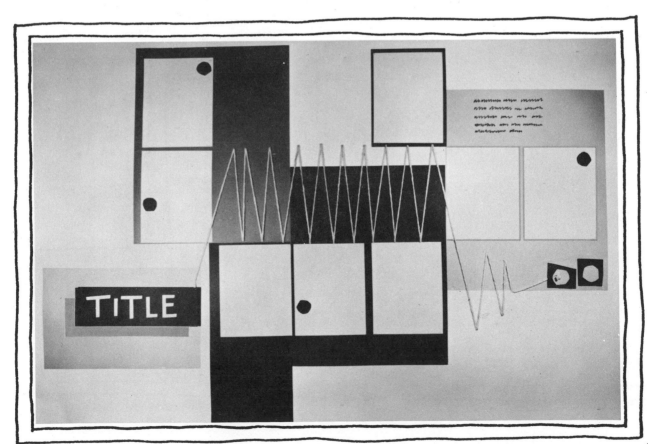

Title raised and yarn introduced.

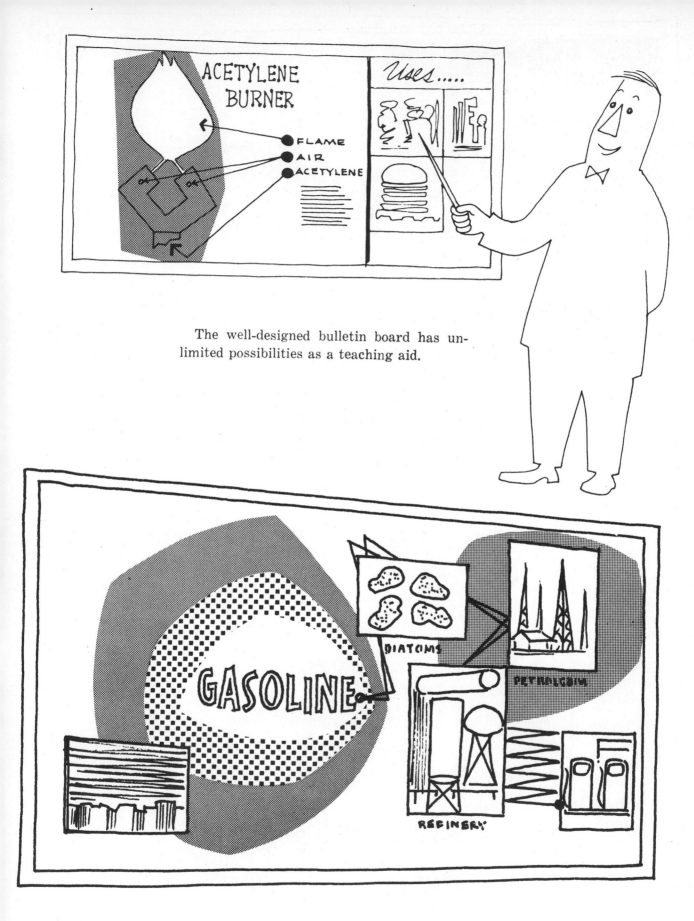

The well-designed bulletin board has un-limited possibilities as a teaching aid.

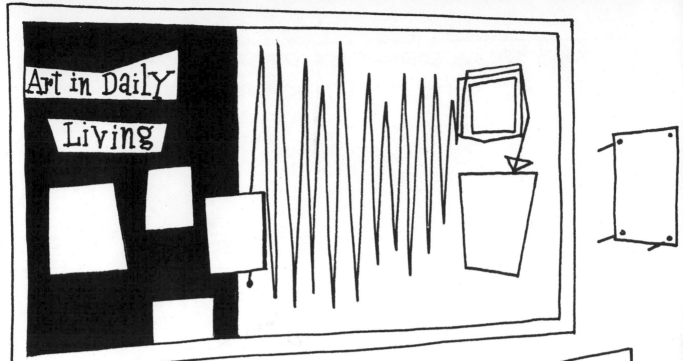

Art in Daily Living

Timely, accurate and unusual illustrative
material is as important as the arrangement.

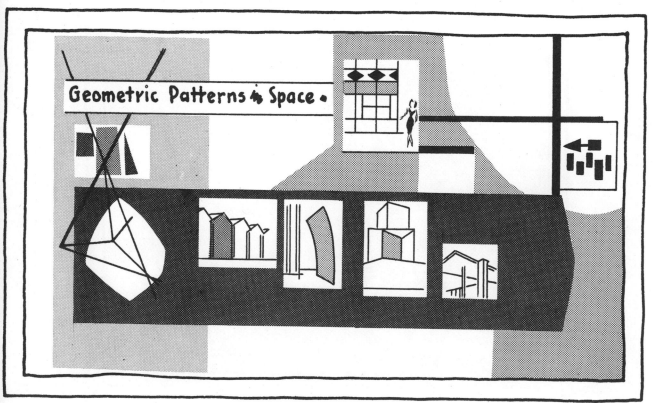

An easel and a homosote board give additional "eye-catching" space for the story on "Wheels."

A significant letter can be used effectively as a background shape.

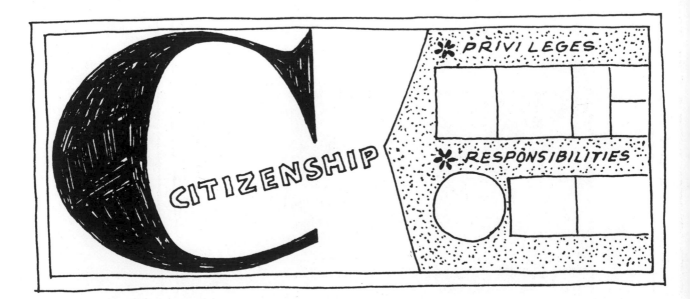

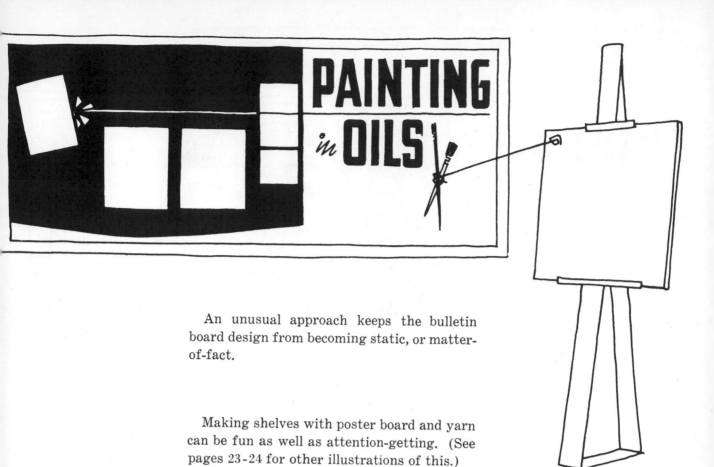

An unusual approach keeps the bulletin board design from becoming static, or matter-of-fact.

Making shelves with poster board and yarn can be fun as well as attention-getting. (See pages 23-24 for other illustrations of this.)

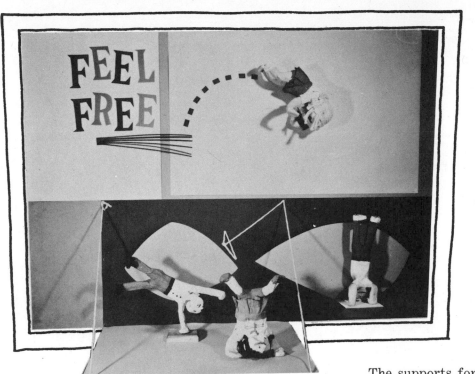

The supports for shelves should be strong enough to ensure holding the 3-D objects being displayed.

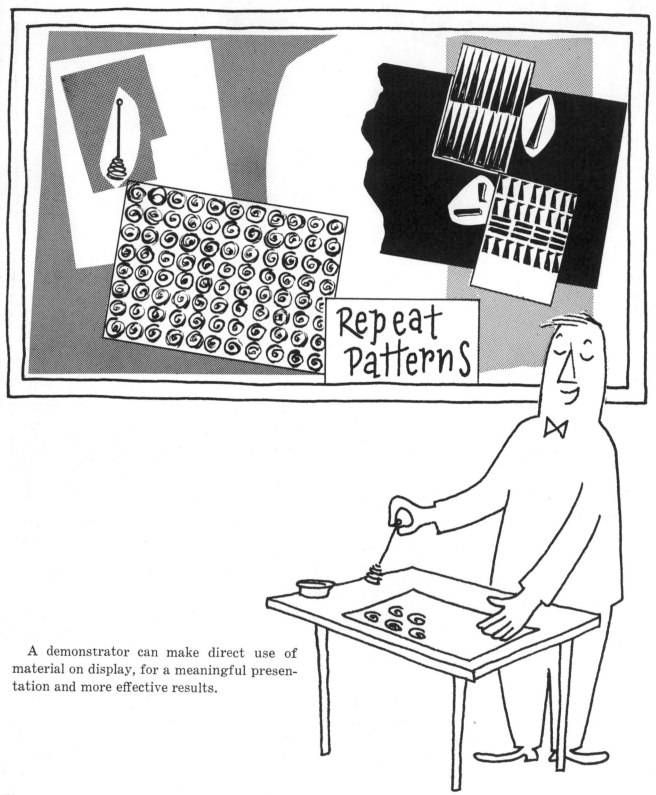

A demonstrator can make direct use of material on display, for a meaningful presentation and more effective results.

Bulletin boards should be kept "alive" by constant exploration of new ideas, materials, and techniques; and by frequent changes in scene.